Here Is the Arctic Winter

Madeleine Dunphy

ILLUSTRATED BY

Alan James Robinson

HYPERION BOOKS FOR CHILDREN

NEW YORK

Text ©1993 by Madeleine Dunphy.
Illustrations ©1993 by Alan James Robinson.
All rights reserved.
Printed in Italy.
For more information address
Hyperion Books for Children,
114 Fifth Avenue, New York, New York 10011.
FIRST EDITION
1   3   5   7   9   10   8   6   4   2
Library of Congress Cataloging-in-Publication Data

Dunphy, Madeleine.
Here is the Arctic winter/Madeleine Dunphy; illustrated by Alan James Robinson.—1st ed.
p.   cm.
Summary: Cumulative text introduces the animals of the cold white world that is the arctic winter.
ISBN 1-56282-336-1 (trade)—ISBN 1-56282-337-X (lib. bdg.)
[1. Zoology—Arctic regions—Fiction. 2. Stories in rhyme.]
I. Robinson, Alan James, ill. II. Title.
PZ8.3.D9264He   1993
[E]—dc20   92-72022   CIP   AC

The artwork for each picture is done in watercolor.
This book is set in 14-point Caslon No. 224 Book.

For Dermot
—M. D.

For my mother
—A. J. R.

*H*ere is the Arctic winter.

*H*ere is the sky
that is dark day and night,
where the sun does not rise
in this cold world of white:
Here is the Arctic winter.

*H*ere are the wolves

who howl at the sky

that is dark day and night,

where the sun does not rise

in this cold world of white:

Here is the Arctic winter.

*H*ere are the caribou

that flee from the wolves

who howl at the sky

that is dark day and night,

where the sun does not rise

in this cold world of white:

Here is the Arctic winter.

*H*ere is the willow,

which is food for the caribou

that flee from the wolves

who howl at the sky

that is dark day and night,

where the sun does not rise

in this cold world of white:

Here is the Arctic winter.

Here is the hare
that eats the willow,
which is food for the caribou
that flee from the wolves
who howl at the sky
that is dark day and night,
where the sun does not rise
in this cold world of white:
Here is the Arctic winter.

*H*ere is the owl

who chases the hare

that eats the willow,

which is food for the caribou

that flee from the wolves

who howl at the sky

that is dark day and night,

where the sun does not rise

in this cold world of white:

Here is the Arctic winter.

Here is the bear

that is seen by the owl

who chases the hare

that eats the willow,

which is food for the caribou

that flee from the wolves

who howl at the sky

that is dark day and night,

where the sun does not rise

in this cold world of white:

Here is the Arctic winter.

*H*ere is the seal

that dives from the bear

that is seen by the owl

who chases the hare

that eats the willow,

which is food for the caribou

that flee from the wolves

who howl at the sky

that is dark day and night,

where the sun does not rise

in this cold world of white:

Here is the Arctic winter.

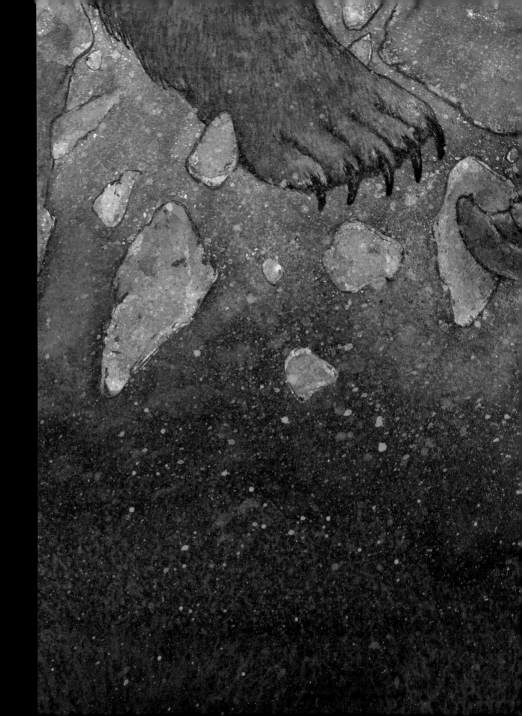

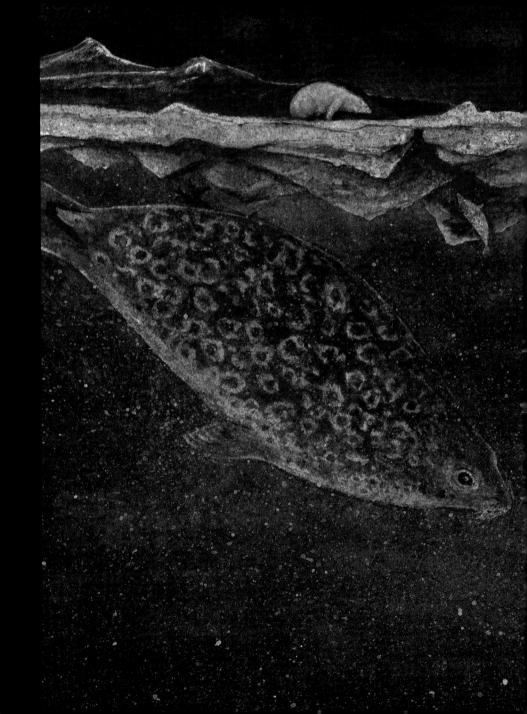

*H*ere are the fish
that swim with the seal
that dives from the bear
that is seen by the owl
who chases the hare
that eats the willow,
which is food for the caribou
that flee from the wolves
who howl at the sky
that is dark day and night,
where the sun does not rise
in this cold world of white:
Here is the Arctic winter.

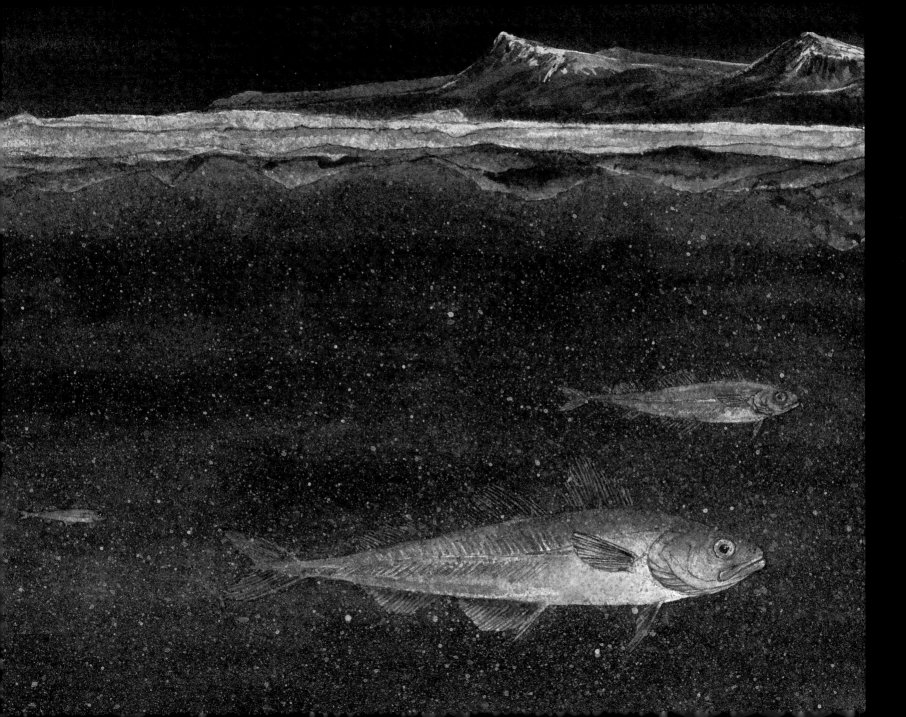

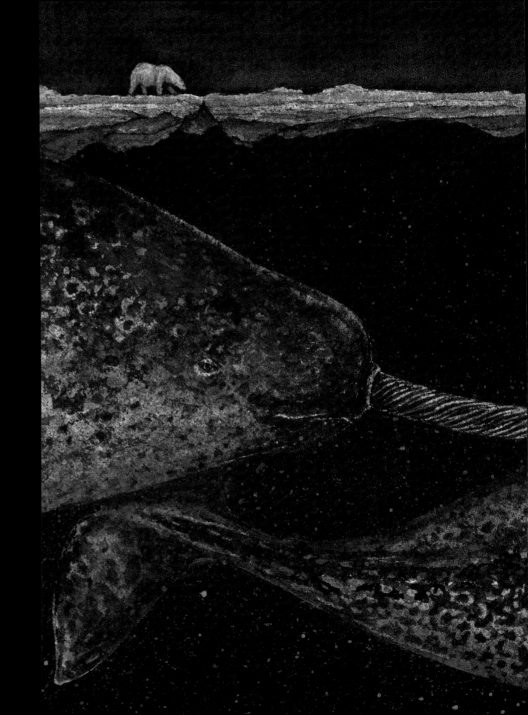

Here is the whale

who eats the fish

that swim with the seal

that dives from the bear

that is seen by the owl

who chases the hare

that eats the willow,

which is food for the caribou

that flee from the wolves

who howl at the sky

that is dark day and night,

where the sun does not rise

in this cold world of white:

Here is the Arctic winter.

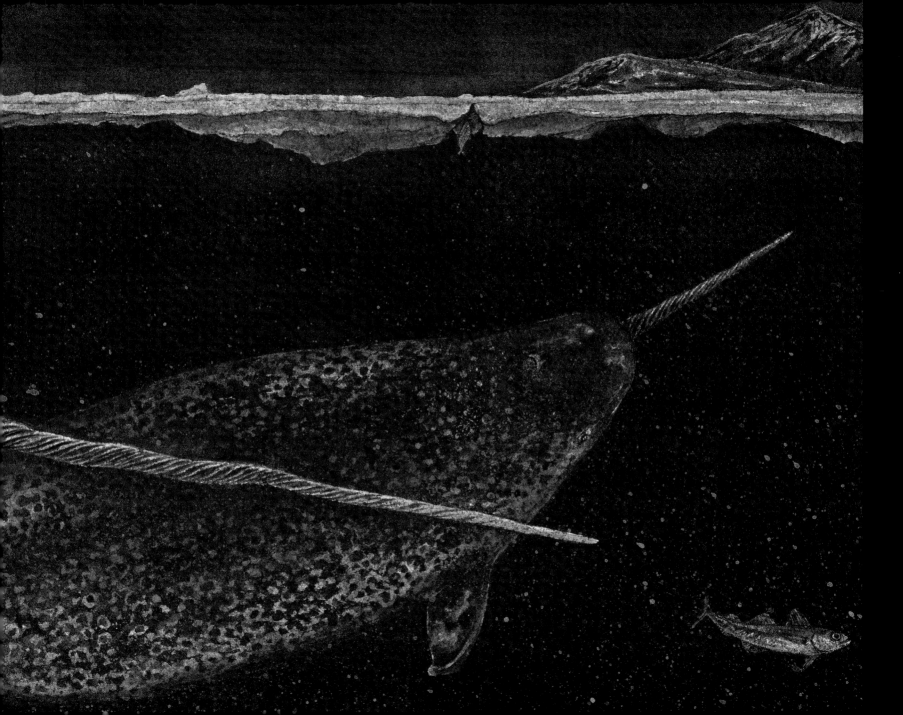

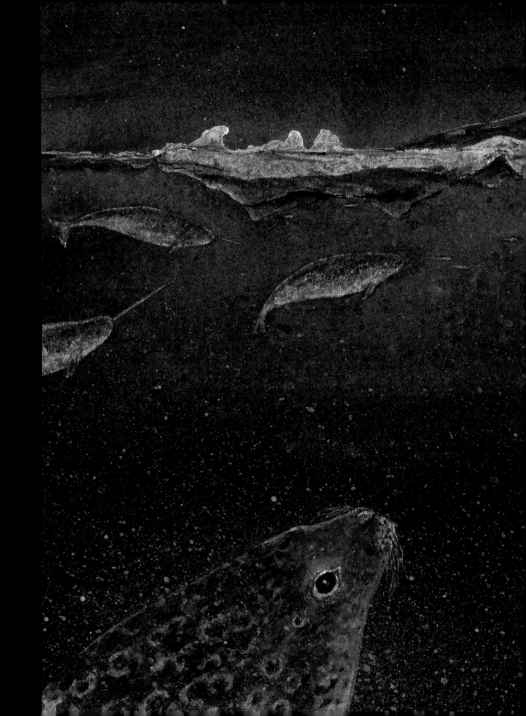

Here is the sea ice

that is above the whale

who eats the fish

that swim with the seal

that dives from the bear

that is seen by the owl

who chases the hare

that eats the willow,

which is food for the caribou

that flee from the wolves

who howl at the sky

that is dark day and night,

where the sun does not rise

in this cold world of white:

Here is the Arctic winter.

*H*ere are the northern lights,

which reflect on the sea ice

that is above the whale

who eats the fish

that swim with the seal

that dives from the bear

that is seen by the owl

who chases the hare

that eats the willow,

which is food for the caribou

that flee from the wolves

who howl at the sky

that is dark day and night,

where the sun does not rise

in this cold world of white:

Here is the Arctic winter.

*H*ere is the sky

that shines with the northern lights,

which reflect on the sea ice

that is above the whale

who eats the fish

that swim with the seal

that dives from the bear

that is seen by the owl

who chases the hare

that eats the willow,

which is food for the caribou

that flee from the wolves

who howl at the sky

that is dark day and night,

where the sun does not rise

in this cold world of white:

Here is the Arctic winter.

The animals shown below live in the Arctic all year long. They are hardy enough to survive the Arctic's cold and dark winter. There are many animals that would not survive the cold and dark. They migrate south for the winter but then return for the summer. Arctic summers are much warmer, and the sun shines day and night.

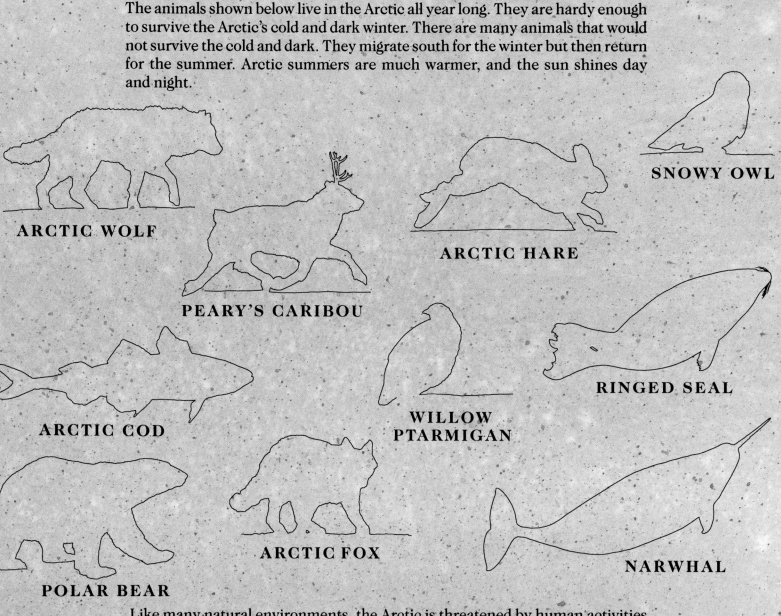

ARCTIC WOLF

PEARY'S CARIBOU

ARCTIC HARE

SNOWY OWL

ARCTIC COD

WILLOW PTARMIGAN

RINGED SEAL

POLAR BEAR

ARCTIC FOX

NARWHAL

Like many natural environments, the Arctic is threatened by human activities. If you would like to find out ways to help protect the Arctic, you can write to the National Audubon Society, Arctic Program, RR1, Box 171, Sharon, Connecticut 06069.